Toasters

Toasters

Elaine Marie Alphin

Carolrhoda Books, Inc./Minneapolis

The photographs in this book are reproduced through the courtesy of: IPS, cover (top middle and lower left), pp. 3, 6 (both), 8, 9, 10 (bottom), 16 (top), 17, 20 (bottom), 35, 42, 43, 44 (top), 47; National Housewares Manufacturers Association, James Beck, photographer, cover (top right), pp. 5, 25, 30, 38 (top); Black & Decker, cover (middle right), p. 13; UPI/Corbis-Bettmann, cover (bottom right), p. 33 (top); Hall of Electrical History of the Schenectady Museum Association, Schenectady, NY, cover (middle left), pp. 19 (bottom), 20 (top), 21 (bottom), 24, 31 (both); Brown Brothers, pp. 1, 19 (top), 21 (top); Provided by Sunbeam Corporation, all rights reserved, p. 2; Photo Researchers, Inc., pp. 7 (bottom) (©Biophoto Ass./S.S.), 33 (bottom) (©Aaron Haupt), 36 (©Charles D. Winters); Eliot Elisofon, Eliot Elisofon Archives, National Museum of African Art, Smithsonian Institution, p. 7 (top); Archive Photos, pp. 10 (top), 16 (bottom), 18, 28 (bottom), 29; John Erste, pp. 11, 12, 44 (bottom), 45 (all); Minnesota Historical Society, pp. 14, 22; Winterthur Museum, p. 15 (bottom); Stanley B. Burns, M.D. and the Burns Archive, p. 15 (top); U.S. Patent Office, p. 23; Toastmaster Inc., p. 27; Gaslight Advertising Archives pp. 24, 28 (top), 46; DeLonghi America, Inc., p. 32; Hammacher Schlemmer, p. 34 (both); Dennis Gephardt, p. 37 (top); © Toaster Museum, p. 37 (bottom); Allen Memorial Art Museum, Oberlin College, loan from the Estate of Ellen H. Johnson, 1992, p. 38 (bottom); Photofest, pp. 39, 40 (top); Philips Nederland BV, p. 40 (bottom); CALVIN AND HOBBES ©1986 Watterson. Dist. by UNIVERSAL PRESS SYNDICATE. Reprinted by permission. All rights reserved, p. 41.

For Art, who brought a collectible toaster to our marriage. I contributed the toaster oven.

Can you find the United States president on the cover of this book? Harry S. Truman, president from 1945 to 1953, is in the lower right corner, helping his wife, Bess, fix breakfast in 1944.

Words that appear in **bold** in the text are listed in the glossary on page 46.

Carolrhoda Books, Inc., c/o The Lerner Publishing Group
241 First Avenue North, Minneapolis, MN 55401 U.S.A.
Website address: www.lernerbooks.com

Library of Congress Cataloging-in-Publication Data

Alphin, Elaine Marie.
    Toasters / Elaine Marie Alphin.
        p.   cm. — (Household history)
    Includes index.
    Summary: Presents the history and development of this household appliance, describes how it works, and discusses its role in popular culture: includes recipes using a toaster.
    ISBN 1-57505-243-1
    1. Electric toasters—History—Juvenile literature. [1. Electric toasters.] I. Title. II. Series.
TX657.T58A47 1998
641.5'89—dc21   97-34328

Manufactured in the United States of America
1 2 3 4 5 6 – JR – 03 02 01 00 99 98

Contents

Toasted bread is a quick breakfast food.

No More Moldy Bread

Oh no! You've overslept and the school bus will be at your corner in 15 minutes! There's no time for a hot breakfast—or is there?

Drop two slices of bread or an English muffin in your **toaster** while you get dressed. Warm, golden toast will be ready when you race back into the kitchen. Spread on some jam or melt a little cheese between the slices. You can head to the bus stop with time to spare—and with a hot breakfast to get you ready for the day ahead.

A toaster can help you get a flying start on a day. It's also a tool for keeping one of your favorite foods healthy for you. The grains that are in bread fill you up and give you energy.

Since prehistoric times, people have eaten grain. First they ground it up and ate it raw. Then they learned to stir water into the grain and bake it. Early loaves of bread were really flat platters of grain and water.

Then someone in Egypt discovered that leaving this dough in a warm place before baking made something special happen. **Yeast** in the air settled on the dough. Yeast is actually a moist, yellowish fungus that makes molecules in dough break down. The yeast mixes with the sugar in the flour and forms tiny gas bubbles. These bubbles can't escape the dough, so they puff it up.

A woman bakes lightly puffed bread in a traditional Egyptian oven.

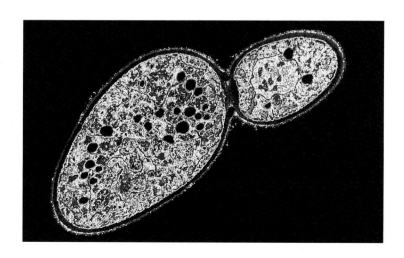

The yeast that makes bread rise, magnified 2,700 times

Above: In the former Soviet state of Moldova, a man prepares to carry home fresh-baked bread.

Opposite page: Moldy bread

That Egyptian cook was probably surprised to see the ball of dough double in size! And after the dough baked, the result wasn't the flat, hard bread people were used to eating. Instead, the loaf of bread that came out of the oven was lighter and almost fluffy. As the bread cooked, the bubbles finally popped and the gas disappeared. But the puffed-up dough had already started baking, and it held its puffed-up shape.

Preserving the Staff of Life

Bread was the main food for many people in ancient times. People depended on it. They could not be sure what they might find by hunting, but they could plant grain and be certain that they could bake bread. Bread was so important that some people even paid for things using bags of grain or loaves of bread as money!

But there was one problem with bread. If it wasn't eaten within a few days of being baked, it started to look and taste strange. Fuzzy green or gray **mold** would grow on it.

Mold is a fungus that floats in the air as microscopic **spores.** Each spore is a life-form, looking for a place to grow. The yeast that landed on the bread dough was also carried in spores.

The moist dough was a good place for the yeast to grow. The heat of baking popped the bubbles in the dough and released the gas from the fungus. This made the bread safe to eat. Fresh bread is moist also, and it offers a good home to other types of spores, including mold. Eating moldy bread, however, can make kids and their parents sick.

In ancient times, the best way to keep bread from molding was to dry it. And the best way to dry bread and still keep it tasty was to toast it. Spores could fall on toasted bread without making it moldy. Toasted bread would keep far longer than a few days. It could easily be carried on a trip and made a crunchy meal that was almost as good as bread fresh out of the oven.

Egyptians looked for ways to prevent bread from molding. Covering it with a cloth helped, but microscopic spores could sift through the weave of the cloth and infest the bread. People could bake small batches of bread every day at home. This way they would eat the bread before it got moldy. An army or a hunting expedition might not be able to bake regularly, however. To keep their bread fresh while they traveled, toasting was the answer.

Many early electric toasters had to be carefully watched to avoid burnt bread.

Although the Egyptians didn't realize it, toasting bread caused a chemical change. At about 310 degrees Fahrenheit, sugars and starches in bread start to **caramelize,** or turn brown. This chemical change also heightens the flavor of these sugars and starches, so that plain toast is tastier than plain bread. The catch is that when bread gets much hotter than 310 degrees Fahrenheit, sugars and grain fibers start to **carbonize**—they blacken and burn.

Burnt toast

What Makes Toasters Tick

Modern electric toasters make it easy to toast bread without burning it. Pop-up toasters are designed with slots for individual slices of bread. Racks inside these slots hold the bread upright. When you place a piece of bread in the slot and push down the handle, the rack lowers the bread between two **heating elements.** When the rack locks into place at the bottom of the toaster, a catch pushes a switch that lets electricity flow through the heating elements.

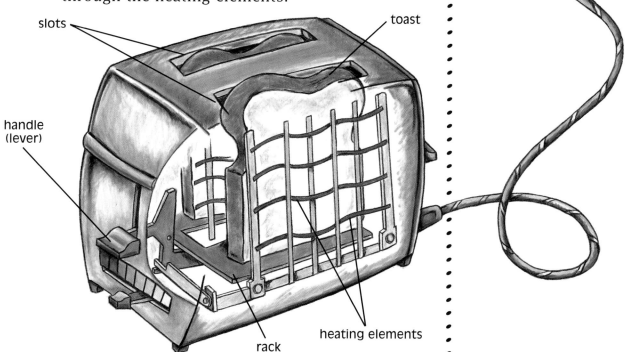

slots

toast

handle (lever)

rack

heating elements

If you only want one piece of toast but you don't drop your bread in the slot marked "one slice," are you breaking a rule? Will the toaster blow up? No, but your toast may take longer and may pop up a bit blackened. The bimetallic timer strip is located in the "one slice" slot. A single slice of bread placed in the other slot could burn before enough heat seeps over and trips the timer.

These heating elements are made of thin wires of nickel-chromium **alloy** woven between strips of mica. As electricity flows into them, the wires glow red hot, toasting the slice of bread. A strip of **bimetal** near the heating elements acts as a timer. When the wires heat up, one side of the bimetallic timer strip heats and expands, while the other side does not.

The strip gets hotter until it bends and touches a **trip plate.** Touching that trip plate cuts off the electric flow and lets the rack pop up. If you turn the control to a darker setting, this moves the timer strip farther away from the heating element so that the strip takes longer to bend. Turning to a lighter setting moves the timer strip closer to the heat so that it bends more quickly.

handle (lever)

browning control

heating element

rack

bimetallic timer strip

trip plate

Modern toaster ovens can fit into small spaces.

Toaster ovens operate much the same way, although they have more space than pop-up toasters do. A toaster oven has a door in front that opens to allow the cook to slide a rack in and out. Toaster ovens offer extra cooking possibilities. They come with wire racks for toasting and solid metal racks for cooking. The heating elements are positioned above and below the rack, and a control allows you to choose between toasting, baking, and broiling.

But ancient Egyptians were toasting bread long before pop-up toasters and toaster ovens were invented. How did they toast their bread to a perfect golden brown?

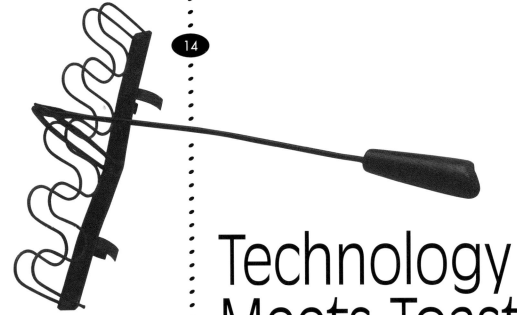

This type of iron toasting rack sat near the coals of an open fire.

Technology Meets Toast

Ever since the first yeast spores puffed up Egyptian bread dough in 2600 B.C.—and ever since the first mold spores spoiled that bread—cooks have been toasting bread to keep it healthy. In the beginning, people toasted bread the same way you toast marshmallows. They poked a sharpened stick into a piece of bread and held it over a fire.

Just as marshmallows get black on one side and undercooked on the other, bread didn't toast evenly. Sometimes the stick began to burn and the cook had to start again. And, just like a marshmallow, sometimes a slice fell into the fire.

Even if the toast could be pulled out before it went up in flames, it would be dirty and sooty.

Because toasted bread stayed fresh longer when people were traveling, toast was on the move. When the Romans arrived in Egypt in the 50s B.C., they discovered toast. When their armies invaded Britain in the year A.D. 44, they took toast with them. Soon toast became a popular way of preserving bread all across Europe.

With the increased use of metal tools, the toasting process improved. People used metal prongs to hold their bread more securely. As the metal got hotter, these **toasting forks** even toasted the bread from the inside. But there was still no way to toast the surface of the bread evenly to seal out mold. Toast, and toasting technology, did not change greatly for many centuries.

Toasting took on new meaning in the 1700s. People would drop pieces of spiced toast into drinks to make them taste better. When a gentleman wanted to impress a lady, he would drink to her, saying that her name did more to make the drink taste good than any toast could. This led to the phrase "to toast" someone.

Above: An early American toasting fork
Above, right: Women toast to their health in the 1800s.

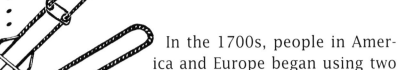

In the 1700s, people in America and Europe began using two long toasting forks instead of one. The handles of these forks were hinged like tongs. The prongs held the bread firmly between them rather than spearing the bread. No more falling off into the fire!

This invention inspired blacksmiths to think of better ways to hold bread securely. Every village smithy offered its own toaster. Usually this was a pair of racks made of thin metal strips. The cook placed a slice of bread on the lower rack, then latched the lower rack to the upper rack. This way, the cook could turn the toast easily and avoid burning the bread.

Tin Toasters & Towers

After wood and coal stoves replaced open fires for cooking in the mid-1800s, people had to find new ways of toasting bread. Earlier toasting racks had worked because the metal conducted the fire's heat to the bread. Inventors looked at ways to adapt this to a cookstove. They developed tin and wire toasters that could stand on top of the stove. The stove would heat the wire, and the wire would toast the bread.

The Bromwell Wire Goods Company of Michigan City, Indiana, was the first manufacturer to mass-produce a "Toaster Oven," as their toaster was called. This toaster looked like a sloping tin tower. It narrowed at the top, with wire racks to hold bread that leaned in toward the center. The cook's hands were free to do other things, but the toaster had to be watched carefully. One side of the bread toasted at a time, and the bread had to be taken out of the rack and turned before that side burned. The toaster kept the done side warm as it slowly toasted the other side.

Pyramid-shaped metal toasters (left) could be used on top of early freestanding cookstoves. These cast-iron stoves were made by pouring liquid iron into stove-shaped molds. The resulting stove was strong enough to contain a fire and conducted heat well. The wood or coal fire heated the stove, the cast-iron stove heated the metal toaster, and the metal wires in the toaster heated the bread.

Opposite page, top:
A hinged toaster
Opposite page, bottom:
A toasting rack sits on the floor, near a crackling fire.

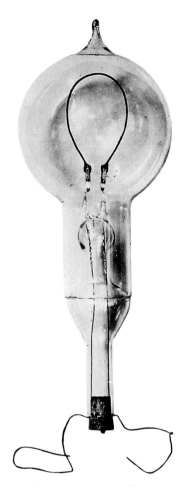

Thomas Alva Edison perfected the first electric light bulb in 1879. A reliable electric toaster took longer to invent.

Electricity revolutionized toasters, although at first it didn't seem that electricity could be used for most appliances. One of the first electric power stations in the world went on-line in New York City in September of 1882—and it only ran from dusk to dawn. This new power source was intended to replace gas to light homes. The electric company reasoned that it only needed to generate power when it was dark. As electric companies spread to more and more towns and cities, companies kept this dusk-to-dawn policy.

Inventors were soon scrambling to find ways of using electricity to power things other than lights. Even before daytime electricity was available, electric cooking ranges and electric irons were being patented.

By 1905 most electric companies were offering 24-hour power. They had expected that businesses would use the power to run motors and generators. But they were amazed at the power used in private homes. Everyone wanted electric appliances to speed up housework.

Over the next few decades, a well-equipped household boasted an electric coffee pot, an electric egg boiler, an electric kettle, and an electric cooker—and this was only to make breakfast!

There were electric dishwashers, mixers, potato peelers, and knife grinders for other tasks in the kitchen, and electric heaters, washing machines, and vacuum cleaners around the house.

It didn't take as much effort to toast a piece of bread as it did to clean a carpet or wash clothes. But earlier cooks had only been able to toast bread when the cookstove or the fireplace was blazing. An electric toaster could be switched on all by itself—certainly an advantage on a hot summer morning.

Turning On the Toaster

General Electric patented the first successful electric toaster in 1910. It looked more like the earlier tin and wire cages than a modern toaster. There was no casing to hide the works, or moving parts. The bare wire skeleton consisted of a rack to hold the bread and a single exposed heating element of nickel wire woven through sheets of mica. The toaster had only one heating element and no heat control, so cooks had to turn the bread by hand when one side was done, just as they had turned it when using a stovetop toaster.

Above: A family enjoys an electric breakfast in the early 1920s. Below: General Electric's first successful electric toaster

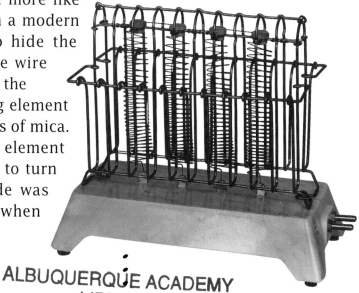

Above: General Electric's early toasters came with a rack for keeping bread warm.

Also in 1910, Westinghouse introduced its Toaster Stove, and the race was on to build a better electric toaster. In the first Westinghouse toaster, the heating element was placed on a raised base. A wire mesh tray lay across the top, and the slice of bread lay on the mesh—much as bread had once been held in a wire cage over a fire. Later versions had doors that sealed off the heating element and opened for putting in bread.

Engineers still looked for ways to cook toast more efficiently. In the 1920s, an unknown inventor introduced the first "flip-flop" toaster. The cook could turn the bread when it was done on one side by lowering a side panel.

Right: A flip-flop toaster

Left: Breakfast with a pivoting toaster
Below: Breakfast with a flip-flop toaster

In 1922 the Estate Stove Company in Hamilton, Ohio, came up with a tidy way to toast four pieces of bread at once. The Estate electric toaster was a square box with the heating element in the center. Wire bread racks pivoted out from the four corners. When the cook turned on the toaster, one side of the bread faced the heating element. Flipping a lever made the racks turn, like flapping wings, so that the other side of the bread faced the heating element.

Making more toast at once was certainly an advantage for a large family, but the cook still had to watch the toast and make sure that it didn't burn. This nagging problem frustrated many inventors as well as household cooks. The solution came from a master mechanic who was also a toast lover.

An early pop-up toaster created by Charles Strite

The End of Burnt Toast

Charles Strite was fed up with burnt toast. During World War I, Strite worked in a manufacturing plant in Stillwater, Minnesota. Company cafeterias can be as unsatisfactory as school cafeterias, and there was one thing about the company food that drove Strite especially crazy. Every morning the breakfast toast was burned. The cooks had too much to do to keep a careful eye on the toast. Strite made up his mind to find a way of toasting bread that didn't depend on human attention.

Strite tackled the problem in his own workshop at home. He reasoned that the toast burned because it was left too long. First he built an adjustable timer that turned the heating element off. However, the heating element stayed hot after the power switched off. The toast could still burn unless it was taken out of the toaster. Someone had to come and remove the toast. Strite was back where he started, trusting busy cooks to pay attention to his toast.

The answer seemed to lie in finding a way for the toaster to take the toast out by itself. Strite experimented with a motor and springs. Then he linked the timer to the springs. Once the timer turned off the heating element, it released the springs and the slice of toast popped up. The only thing the cook had to do was put the bread in the toaster and switch it on. Strite's pop-up toaster did the rest.

Strite patented his toaster in 1919 and formed his own company to produce it. Aware that busy cooks were the ones most likely to forget toast, Strite decided to market his toaster to restaurants. The Childs restaurant chain was interested, and Strite agreed to manufacture one hundred toasters for delivery the following year.

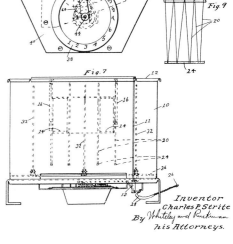

Strite filed his first toaster patent in 1919. It was approved in 1921.

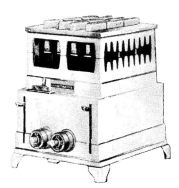

Strite's commercial toaster gradually became a success.

A friend, Glen Waters, bought into the company. Waters offered to pay for Strite's supplies and time while Strite built one hundred toasters by hand for Childs. The toasters were delivered on time—and, one by one, all were returned to Strite because of mechanical flaws.

Each time a toaster came back, Strite tinkered with it until he had it adjusted correctly. When he returned the appliance to the restaurant, it was welcomed back. Cooks and servers had already seen the advantages of an automatic toaster, even though the original hadn't worked perfectly. Restaurant orders continued, but they trickled in slowly. That was good, because Strite's production was slow.

Strite and Waters found another investor in Harold Genter. They changed the company name to the Waters Genter Company and added a crew of factory workers. More and more people wanted electric appliances for the home, and Strite could envision large sales of household toasters. First he needed to find some way to reliably mass-produce his invention, rather than building each one by hand. Strite already had the name: Toastmaster. What he needed was a production manager.

In 1925 the Waters Genter Company hired Murray Ireland as their factory superintendent. Ireland took Strite's original working plans and redesigned them to make the toaster easier for factory workers to build on an efficient production line. Production skyrocketed.

The first Toastmaster household unit was the Model 1A1. It was a blend of Strite's original idea and Ireland's practical experience in managing production. The Model 1A1 was sleek. Its nickel-plated curving lines sloped from the slot to the black control levers. A row of horizontal vents along the side created the illusion of racing speed.

Strite's Toastmaster model 1A1

After the new Toastmaster hit the market, Strite sold his company to Max McGraw. Born in 1883, right after the first power company generated electricity, McGraw was fascinated by this new power source. As a boy, he used money from his horseback newspaper route to take a course in electricity. Seventeen-year-old McGraw soon built a reputation installing electric lights and appliances. Then he began buying companies like Toastmaster and making them profitable.

The toaster was even better inside. While Ireland had streamlined Strite's original design to speed up production, he hadn't skimped on the features that made it work. When the Model 1A1 appeared in 1926, toaster sales jumped to one million a year.

Advertisements for this new automatic toaster promised "perfect toast every time—without watching, without turning, without burning." These claims were exactly what cooks longed to hear, but were they true?

Taming the Toaster

Strite's timer mechanism worked well. But the heating element couldn't cool down completely between pieces of toast.

If a family of three had two slices of toast each for breakfast, the first piece would turn out a little light. But the heating element would still be warm when the second slice of bread was put in. Setting the timer for the same amount of time actually kept the bread hotter longer, and that piece would be a bit darker than the first. By the time the sixth slice was toasted, it would be dark enough that even Strite himself might have called it burned.

You Read . . . while the TOASTMASTER Toasts

NO TOAST TURNING

NO WATCHING

NO BURNT TOAST

This advertisement from 1929 promises an end to burnt toast, but inventors were still working to make each slice a perfect golden brown.

Instructions for the toaster warned people to warm the heating element by running the toaster the first time without any bread in it at all. Then it suggested leaving time in between slices for cooling. By the late 1920s, however, families were in a rush. They expected electric appliances to perform quickly and reliably. No one was willing to wait while a toaster cooled down (and the rest of breakfast got cold).

To sell the Toastmaster, the company hired a sales force of women who went door to door. Saleswomen carried a loaf of bread and a sample toaster. Their motto was "Set it and forget it!"

TOASTMASTER
Can't Forget

Toastmaster's Flexible Toast-Timer is almost human. Whether you start with Toastmaster stone cold or piping hot, the Toast-Timer times each slice to a dot — then shuts off the current. "Only Toastmaster pops up perfect toast every time for everybody."

Toastmaster boasted that its compensated toaster solved the problem of burnt toast.

Electric toasters—with trays full of food— became a fashionable addition to many parties.

Toastmaster engineers kept working on the problem during the 1920s and soon invented a "compensated" toaster. This was the first toaster with a piece of bimetal in the timer circuit. The metal was sensitive to the temperature of the heating element. It compensated for the steady warming of the toaster over several pieces of toast so the last ones weren't overdone.

However, not every piece of bread was the same. Fresher bread was more moist. In the winter, bread would be colder in the morning. The toaster needed to be sensitive to the condition of the bread as well as to the temperature of the heating element.

In 1930 the Proctor Electric Company took the first step toward solving this problem. Proctor made an automatic toaster with a timing strip. The strip could sense the temperature of the bread as well as the temperature inside the slot, between the heating elements. This kept the toast consistently golden brown, no matter how moist or cold the bread was. When the toast was done, the current turned itself off. Different toaster models either rang a bell or flashed a signal light to alert the cook.

Early toasters made up in creative designs what they lacked in controlled toasting. Some manufacturers put different appliances together to do related jobs. People could buy a combination toaster, grill, and percolator—or a toaster and corn popper combination!

A Sunbeam toaster and tray set

Afer World War II, new technology allowed engineers to install a silent temperature sensor in new toasters, doing away with noisy, ticking timers. To the engineers' surprise, cooks weren't pleased with the change. Unless they could hear it ticking, how did they know the toaster was really working? Gradually, cooks began to believe that the new silent toasters worked as well as the prewar models.

Sunbeam Corporation solved the problem of burnt toast once and for all in 1949. Their research and design engineers developed an improved bimetal sensor control. This sensor was more reliable because it was triggered by heat reflecting off the bread itself. The old sensor in the compensated toaster only reacted to the temperature of the heating elements.

Innovations and Ovens

Next the competition turned to ways to make the toaster do more than just toast bread reliably. Westinghouse toasters boasted a lever that raised the bread high enough so that you could remove it without burning your fingers on the hot metal. Other models offered a sliding crumb tray or a hinged bottom that made cleaning easy.

But the greatest innovation was actually a return to the past. The first electric toasters had promised to take the work of making breakfast out of the kitchen and away from the stove. In 1955 General Electric combined toaster and stove in its Toast-R-Oven.

The Toast-R-Oven featured a pop-up toaster mounted above a warming drawer. The heating element could either toast the bread above, or it could heat something placed in the drawer below. People used this early version to warm rolls or buns. Engineers at General Electric saw the possibilities of using the toaster's heating elements to actually bake, as the appliance's name suggested.

In 1961 General Electric produced its first true toaster oven. The vertical toaster slot was turned sideways. This allowed the heating elements to heat the oven compartment beneath the toaster more effectively. This oven not only warmed food that was already cooked, but it could also bake on its own. And it could prepare the frozen TV dinners that had become popular. It was so successful that General Electric produced a king-size version in 1971 with greater cooking space.

The Toast-R-Oven combined toasting and warming.

A king-size toaster oven from General Electric

Modern toaster ovens allow families to bake, grill, and toast without turning on the main oven.

Cooks loved the idea of combining toaster and oven. New inventions can be a trade-off, however. The better the ovens got, the less effective the toaster itself became. Larger cooking compartments meant that toasters could handle thick bagels and muffins. But thinner slices of bread were farther away from the upper heating element than the lower one. Unless it was turned by hand, the bread would be toasted unevenly. The wire rack that held the bread left scorched stripes on the bottom of the toast.

Despite these problems, the toaster oven could turn a plain piece of toast into a meal. Families melted toppings like cheese onto bread after it was browned. The greatest advantage of the toaster oven was that it allowed kids to heat up leftovers, broil a burger, or grill a toasted sandwich without having to turn on the main oven.

The Competition Heats Up

When the first household **microwave oven** appeared in 1952, it was far too expensive for most families. But as prices came down, the microwave presented a serious threat to the toaster oven. If a pop-up toaster could make toast and a microwave could warm up leftovers and even

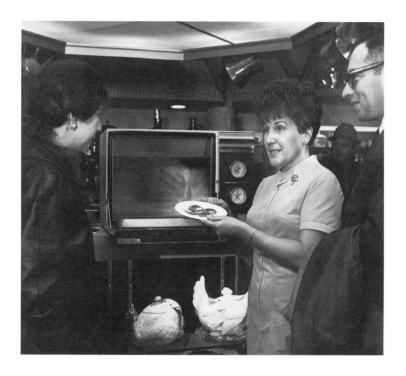

Microwave ovens are great for reheating foods.

cook food from scratch, was the toaster oven a thing of the past?

Not at all—the toaster oven's usefulness lay in the original intentions behind toasting: drying, crisping, and browning. A microwave could cook, but meat looked gray and rolls turned damp and rubbery. The toaster oven could still brown meat, crisp breads, and warm leftover pizza so that it tasted fresh instead of limp.

When cut metal pieces are placed around slices of bread in this toaster, messages and designs appear on the finished toast!

The Hot Diggity Dogger allows people to toast buns while heating hot dogs.

Faced with competition from toaster ovens and microwave ovens, toaster makers looked for ways to make pop-up toasters do their original job even better. In the 1990s, computer microchips were even used to make toast. Programmable computerized toasters automatically center thin slices of bread or thick bagels. These toasters can be programmed for up to three different settings. This makes toasting easier if your parents like dark toast and you like yours light, or if someone in your family regularly toasts waffles instead of bread.

Toasters of Tomorrow

In the future, household appliances may all be controlled by a central computer. Imagine getting ready to leave school and being able to send home instructions by computer for your toaster oven to start heating that leftover pizza!

In some crowded kitchens, technology is less important than saving space. Black & Decker pioneered the concept of space-saving tools and then applied it to a toaster that mounts under a cabinet. The appliance is smaller than a toaster oven, but it has a little extra space to handle rolls and pastries. The toaster unit is insulated, so it won't scorch the cabinet as it heats up. It also features an **infrared** heating element that uses the penetrating heat of red rays of light beyond the visible spectrum, rather than the usual glowing nickel-chromium wire and sheets of mica.

Charles Strite would be delighted at the wealth of machines that have been invented to produce perfect toast. He'd probably also be surprised at how people have taken toasters to their hearts.

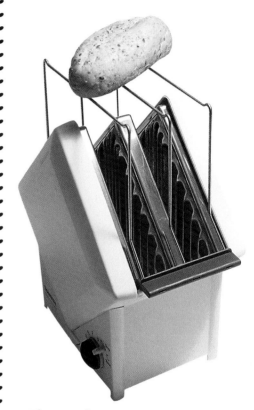

This modern toaster includes a bun warming rack.

Plastic wrapping seals out most of the spores that can cause bread to mold.

All the Comforts of Home

Originally toasting was a way to preserve bread for a longer shelf life. But modern bread often includes preservatives that slow or prevent the growth of spores. Plastic packaging seals out much of the air so that spores have trouble reaching bread in the first place.

Even though kids no longer need to toast bread to keep it mold-free, families still use toasters. Why? Toasted bread tastes great. Hot toast also conjures up visions of parents and grandparents fixing breakfast or late-night snacks of cinnamon toast. For many people, toast generates a sense of comfort, and the toaster itself is a memory they want to keep.

Toasted bread, scraped and arranged like mosaic tiles, is used by artist Dennis Gephardt of Florida.

A display of toasters

Some collectors decorate their houses with toasting forks, stovetop toasters, and early electric toasters. Dealers restore old toasters for collectors—and prices can be steep. Restored chrome toasters sell for thousands of dollars. People's love of old toasters is so strong that manufacturers such as Hamilton Beach, Proctor-Silex, and Sunbeam offer new toasters that are designed to look *old.* These new models look like toasters built in the 1930s and 1940s!

Sleek American electric toasters are part of many museum collections specializing in design.

Claes Oldenburg draws inspiration from the toaster in this sculpture.

Early American-made toasters were unique because they did not look like products designed in Europe, where an elaborate, ornamented style was popular. The sleek chrome of American toasters was free of cluttering swirls and ornaments. It seemed to symbolize the modern age of swift and efficient mechanization.

Toasters are part of many museum collections. Seattle, Washington, once had an entire museum dedicated to the toaster. Visitors to the Toaster Museum could see over two hundred different models. Claes Oldenburg's sculpture, called "Soft Toaster," is one of several toaster-related works of art on display at museums.

The Brave Little Toaster battles with a frog.

Toaster Tales, Tunes, and Talk

Toasters represent both a comforting part of family life and a way for kids to assert their independence by making snacks or breakfast. The toaster is such a familiar figure in our homes that it has found its way into stories and films.

In Thomas M. Disch's *The Brave Little Toaster*, a group of appliances, with the toaster as their leader, decide to search for the boy who owns them. At the story's climax, the loyal toaster sacrifices itself to save its owner—only to be repaired in the final scene to once again pop up perfect toast. The fantasy captures the warmth people feel about their toasters.

For a change of pace, Snoopy prepares piles of toast in A Charlie Brown Thanksgiving.

Breakfast just wouldn't be the same without toasters.

In *A Charlie Brown Thanksgiving*, Snoopy promises to make a holiday dinner for everyone and delivers a big pile of toast. Wallace and Gromit create their own automated toaster in *The Wrong Trousers*. It doesn't just toast bread—it adds jam, too.

Toasters inspire other art forms as well. Heywood Banks sings a popular song called "Toast." On stage Banks taps his drumsticks on a toaster as he sings about the virtues of toasted bread. Johnny Walker even has a song called "The Toast Is Ready."

Toasters have also found their way into our speech: If you leave your skateboard in the driveway and Dad takes a fall, you know you're "toast." On the other hand, if you're the most popular kid in class or in town, you're the "toast of the town."

Toasters pop up everywhere. Berkeley Systems has a popular computer screen saver that features squadrons of toasters flapping wings as they soar through the night sky—ejecting perfect slices of toast as they go.

You may not always care if your toast is a little underdone or if the crust is a bit burned, as Charles Strite did. But being able to fix your own

breakfast or warm up a fast snack without your parents' help is a terrific freedom. So next time you grab a waffle from your toaster, or reheat a slice of pizza or cook a toasted cheese sandwich in your toaster oven, be glad that Strite lost his temper over burnt toast. Otherwise, you might still be flipping your toast by hand—or forgetting to flip it in time and getting stuck with carbonized bread for breakfast.

Calvin, from the cartoon Calvin and Hobbes, *explores the mysteries of the toaster.*

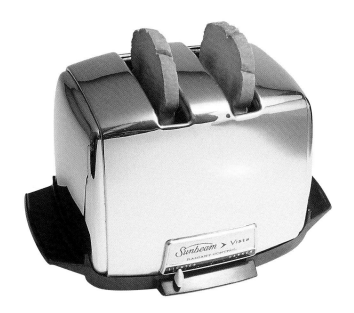

You Will Need:

for cinnamon toast

measuring spoons

1 teaspoon cinnamon

2 tablespoons brown sugar

small bowl

spoon

2 slices bread

table knife

butter or margarine

Tasty Toaster Treats

Cinnamon sugar is a favorite topping for hot, buttered toast:

1. Measure 1 teaspoon cinnamon and 2 tablespoons brown sugar. Place both in a small bowl. Stir with a spoon to mix well.

2. Place each bread slice in a toaster slot. Set toaster to golden brown or medium setting.

3. When toast pops up, use a knife to spread butter or margarine on each slice.

4. Put a spoonful of cinnamon sugar in the middle of each buttered slice of toast. Use the knife to spread mixture over the whole surface. Eat your toast while it's warm! Store extra cinnamon sugar in a sealed container.

Cinnamon toast

Toaster Tips

Do you like buttered toast? Well, don't butter the bread *before* you put it in the toaster. The hot butter could start a fire!

When bread is stuck in the toaster, don't reach in for it. You'll end up with burned fingers. And don't use a metal knife to pry it out—you could get an electric shock! Unplug the toaster and use a wooden spoon handle to rescue your toast.

Don't turn the toaster on if it's close to curtains, newspapers, or a roll of paper towels. The toaster's heating element is meant for toast, but it can set fire to nearby objects.

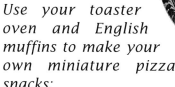

Use your toaster oven and English muffins to make your own miniature pizza snacks:

You Will Need:

for miniature pizzas

English muffins

fork

can opener

15-ounce can prepared pizza sauce

pot holder or oven mitt

spoon

dried basil

sliced mushrooms

chopped onion

chopped green, yellow, or red pepper

grated mozzarella cheese

1. Split muffins in half using a fork. Place muffin halves on toaster oven rack. Plug in toaster oven and turn it on. Toast until muffins turn golden brown. Remember to check muffins so they do not burn. Your toaster oven will not pop them up when they're done!

2. While muffins toast, use can opener to open can of pizza sauce.

3. Open toaster oven using pot holders or oven mitts. Remove toasted muffins.

4. Spoon pizza sauce over muffin halves. Use rounded bottom of spoon to spread sauce evenly. Add a dash of dried basil on top of sauce if you like.

5. Ask an adult to slice and chop vegetables if necessary. Then top your pizza with mushroom slices. Add chopped onion, chopped peppers, or anything else you'd like. Sprinkle grated mozzarella cheese on top of your pizza.

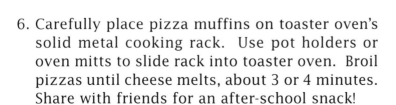

6. Carefully place pizza muffins on toaster oven's solid metal cooking rack. Use pot holders or oven mitts to slide rack into toaster oven. Broil pizzas until cheese melts, about 3 or 4 minutes. Share with friends for an after-school snack!

Glossary

alloy: a mixture of metals in which each metal is melted down and combined with the others to create a new metal with unique properties

bimetal: a piece of metal containing two metals not alloyed together, but side by side, such as the bimetallic strip in a toaster. Each metal behaves according to its own properties. In a toaster, one metal in the strip heats more quickly than the other, causing the strip to bend and turning off the heating element.

caramelize: to change to caramel. In toasting this change makes the sugars and starches in bread turn brown.

carbonize: to change to carbon or to burn. In toasting this chemical change causes flammable objects, such as the sugars and grains in bread, to heat to the point of burning and blackening.

heating elements: thin wires that are warmed by electricity. These wires are woven between strips of mica and conduct heat to a slice of bread in a toaster.

infrared: radiant energy that we cannot see, since the red rays are beyond the visible spectrum of light

microwave oven: a cooking appliance that heats food by applying an electromagnetic wave instead of by conducting heat through electric power or through open flames

mold: a fungus, or plant without roots or leaves, that floats in the air in search of a place to grow. When mold grows on bread, it can make you ill.

spores: very small organisms formed by plants, fungi, and bacteria. These airborne life-forms search for warm, moist places to live. Spores carry both beneficial life-forms, such as yeast, and life-forms that can make you ill, such as mold.

toaster: a device that uses heat to remove moisture from slices of bread and make their surfaces brown and crisp

toaster oven: a small cooking appliance that uses different settings to bake food, broil food, and toast slices of bread or thicker bread products such as muffins or bagels

toasting fork: a long-handled device with metal prongs used to hold slices of bread over an open fire for toasting

trip plate: a device that triggers an alarm or other mechanism. In a toaster, the device causes toasting to end and the rack to pop up.

yeast: yellowish, moist fungus that causes fermentation (the breakdown of molecules in organic compounds such as food). In bread dough, yeast acts to make the bread rise.

Opposite page: Toast towers above a Toastmaster toaster.
Right: The toaster's familiar shape was used for this salt-and-pepper set.

Index